More in the My Fat Fox Earth Art Apps collection, available from Amazon and other bookstores

A portion of the proceeds from all our Earth Apps colouring books will be donated to organizations working to ensure the survival of endangered species by protecting and preserving their natural environments and where necessary through conservation breeding. Each book has more details of which organization it supports and what proportion of the proceeds will be donated.

Endangered Lizards Colouring Book - Illustrated by Jay Manchand

Colour to Save the Ocean – Book One - Illustrated by Kasia Niemczynska

Colour to Save the Ocean – Book Two - Illustrated by Kasia Niemczynska

Color and Save the Ocean – Book One - Illustrated by Karin Hoppe Holloway

Color Funny Doodles – Book One – Humorous - Illustrated by Hartmut Jager

Color Funny Doodles – Book Two – Beautiful - Illustrated by Hartmut Jager

Endangered Animals Colouring Book: UK Amphibians and Reptiles - Illustrated by Cassie Herschel-Shorland

All soon (2015) to be available as apps for mobile devices.

Also available from My Fat Fox

Where Do Swallows Go? – written and illustrated by Cassie Herschel-Shorland

Winter Solstice - a novel by Dan Wright

Please visit www.myfatfox.co.uk for competitions, news and information on our latest publications.

A note on spelling – My Fat Fox is based in the UK but has roots in the USA. Our authors and artists come from several different countries so we sometimes use British English spelling and sometimes US English spelling, depending on their preference.

Endangered Frogs
Colouring Book

Supporting
Save the Frogs!
www.savethefrogs.com/

Written and illustrated by
Jay Manchand

An Earth Apps Book
My Fat Fox Ltd
MMXV

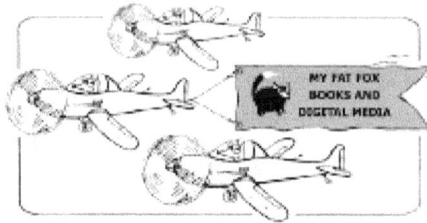

My Fat Fox Ltd
86 Gladys Dimson House
London E7 9DF
United Kingdom
www.myfatfox.co.uk

Endangered Frogs Colouring Book
© 2015 Jay Manchand

www.environment.myfatfox.co.uk/jay_manchand.html

Cover design
© 2015 Jay Manchand and Hartmut Jager

http://hartmut–jager.artistwebsites.com/

ISBN 978-1-905747-45-0

For Chris

"The good life is one inspired by love
and guided by knowledge"

~BERTRAND RUSSELL

About the author

For as long as he can remember, Jay Manchand has had a passion for reptiles and amphibians. His mother would often find him sitting in her pond playing with frogs. Also a keen artist, he has learned to transfer that passion onto paper and canvas. Jay hopes to use his acute attention to detail to encourage others to see the astonishing beauty and intrigue of these underdogs of the animal kingdom.

About 'Save the Frogs!'

'Save the Frogs!' is the world's leading amphibian conservation organization. Their mission is to protect amphibian populations and to promote a society that respects and appreciates nature and wildlife.

They work in California, across the USA and around the world to prevent the extinction of amphibians and to create a better planet for humans.

One third of the profits from sales of this book will be donated to 'Save the Frogs!'.

CONTENTS

You can become a citizen amphibian researcher!

Omaha's Doorly Zoo and Aquarium

Amphibian Conservation Education Project training programs

http://www.omahazoo.com/conservation/amphibian/global-crisis/

To help all endangered amphibians

The Amphibian Survival Alliance

www.amphibians.org

Donations: www.amphibians.org/take-action/

WHAT IS A FROG?

Frogs belong to a class of animals called amphibians. There are three different orders of amphibians: toads, newts and salamanders. Frogs are the largest order of this class with almost 5,000 recorded species.

Amphibians live two lives. The first begins in water as a larvae and is often called a tadpole. As the tadpole develops, it loses its gills and tail and grows lungs and limbs so that it may spend the second part of its life on land.

Most frogs are insect-eating animals. However, larger species of frogs may eat small mammals, lizards and even other frogs.

Frogs spend much of their adult lives on land and are particularly lively at night when they hunt their prey. Frogs are cold-blooded and soft bodied with smooth, moist skin. This means they depend on their environment to regulate their body temperature.

Some frogs have excellent camouflage which helps them to hide. Others have a range of bright colours and bizarre skin patterns that ward off large predators, such as birds, mammals and reptiles, as this warns them that the frog has poisonous skin. Some non-toxic frogs even mimic the colours of toxic frogs. Some frogs use bright colours to attract females during their breeding season when the males will partake in displays of croaking, waving and wrestling with other males for a female's affection. Once mating has taken place, eggs will be laid in or near water where they will develop from tadpoles to frogs and begin the cycle once more.

Frog Life Cycle

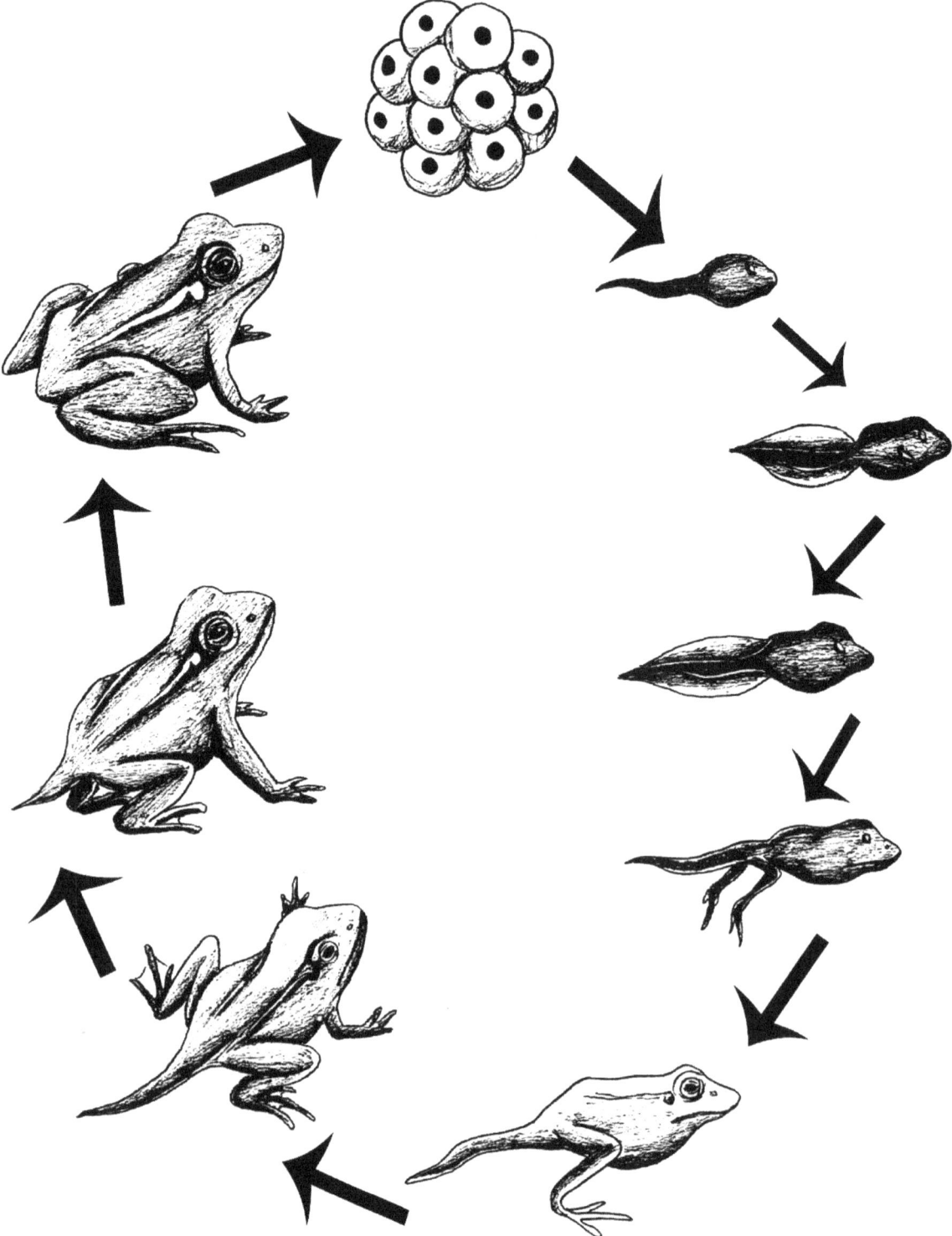

WHY ARE FROGS IN DANGER?

Since 1980 almost 120 species of Amphibians, including frog species, have disappeared and over 1,800 more face extinction. With entire species being rapidly wiped out, this is the largest rate of extinction since the dinosaurs. Frogs are an integral part of nature as both predator and prey. They complete the cycle of nature.

There are many contributing factors to the decline of frogs. We are responsible for the majority of these factors.

Chytrid Fungus

The biggest and most deadly cause of frog populations decreasing is the chytrid fungus. It has decimated entire species. This disease affects the delicate skin of frogs and usually thrives in the water in their environment. Frogs use their skin to 'breathe' and also to 'drink' and so affected water is absorbed through their skin and contaminates their cells and organs. Contaminated water that tadpoles swim in will undoubtedly kill them and thus any hope of future offspring.

How is the chytrid fungus spread? Frogs are shipped around the world in their millions for human consumption, the pet trade and lab testing. An escapee affected by the chytrid fungus will further spread the disease into whichever ecosystem it enters, and water collected along with frogs may be released into other environments continuing the spread of this fatal disease.

Climate Change

The ever changing climate is also responsible for the decline of frog species. When we burn fossil fuels, drive our cars and cut down forests we are affecting the climate patterns that control our planet's weather due to the amount of carbon dioxide being produced. With unpredictable weather comes unpredictable temperatures and this, in turn, affects frog environments making it hotter, wetter or drier. With climate change altering the humidity of certain environments, the deadly chytrid fungus is able to thrive and grow. For frogs, being susceptible to the smallest change in their ecosystem, climate change has impacted their lives in many ways.

Deforestation

The constant eradication of forests for wood, palm oil and land for human settlement is shortening the range of frog habitats considerably. Without as much space to live in, frogs are becoming competitive for places to live and weaker or smaller species are being forced out of their homes. Simple recycling of papers and woods can help towards reducing the amount of trees being cut down.

Pet Trade

With the popularity of keeping exotic pets growing dramatically, the more 'interesting' or 'attractive' species are being both legally and illegally collected from the wild to sell as pets. Frogs are removed from their habitats in their millions each year to be sold around the world and, with so many species already facing extinction, this is having dangerous impacts on remaining species. If you are interested in keeping a frog as a pet, be sure to ask where it has come from. Captive bred species are a much safer option to avoid the spread of the chytrid fungus and this is also less traumatic for the animal itself than if it is wild caught.

Human Consumption

As a worldwide delicacy, and often considered a powerful aphrodisiac, the US alone imports between 450 million and 1.1 billion frogs' legs each year. With many more European countries favouring this food, billions of frogs are being eaten. The number of wild specimens being collected from the wild is not only wiping out species but the collection of these animals is the biggest cause for spreading the chytrid fungus around the world.

Conservation Status

The term 'endangered' is the conservation status of a species which indicates its population in relation to our saying goodbye to it.

This term covers all of the middle 3 categories below because their population numbers are in flux.

The final category isn't an IUCN, International Union for Conservation of Nature, endangered category but lately it has been used by conservation groups and it gives us hope.

Extinct
Extinct in the Wild

Critically Endangered
Endangered
Vulnerable

Near Threatened
Least Concerned

Recovered/ Comebacks

The drawings in the Earth Apps Collection can be coloured with coloured pencils, crayons, felt tips, and watercolours or with anything you'd like to use, though we advise against using marker pens as they may bleed through to the page below.

For more information about the Earth Apps collection please go to www.environment.myfatfox.co.uk.

Karin Hoppe Holloway

ENDANGERED FROG SPECIES

Black-eared Mantella Frog
(Mantella milotympanum)

Critically Endangered; population decreasing

A semi-nocturnal ground dwelling species, the Black-eared Mantella Frog gains its name from its contrasting black ears and nostrils against its bright orange body. It is the smallest of the Mantella frog species. During its breeding season the female lays her eggs and one or more males will fertilise them. The eggs are then washed by rain into nearby swamps where they will hatch into tadpoles. The threats to this Madagascan species are numerous and include their extraction from the wild for the pet trade, deforestation, fires and human settlement.

These organizations are working to save the Black-eared Mantella Frog:

Amphibian Specialist Group and the Amphibian Survival Alliance

http://www.amphibians.org/

Donations: http://www.amphibians.org/take-action/

Durrell Wildlife Conservation Trust

http://www.durrell.org/conservation/

Donations: http://www.durrell.org/donate/
Specify Black-eared Mantella in the 'Dedicate My Donation' box or donate by phone +44 (0)1534 860060

Madagasikara Voakajy

http://www.madagasikara-voakajy.org/

Donations: voakajy@voakjy.mg

Cainarachi Poison Frog
(Ameerega cainarachi)

Vulnerable; population decreasing

The Cainarachi Poison Frog's bright colours deter predators and warn that it is capable of emitting highly poisonous toxins from its skin. It has a bright red back and head, with yellow striping, and its legs are a deep blue. Males are particularly territorial and will croak loudly to attract females. Once courting has occurred, the male fertilises the eggs and guards them until they hatch into tadpoles. He then carries them on his back to nearby water. While considered vulnerable, and not yet endangered, their population is decreasing because the wet forest habitat in Peru is continually declining due to degradation and deforestation for agricultural purposes.

These organizations are working to save the Cainarachi Poison Frog:

Act for Wildlife

http://www.actforwildlife.org.uk/

Donations: http://www.actforwildlife.org.uk/donate/donate-to-a-project/

Cocha Cashu Biological Station

http://cochacashu.sandiegozooglobal.org/

Donations: http://cochacashu.sandiegozooglobal.org/about-us/how-to-donate/

Golden Poison Arrow Frog
(Atelopus zeteki)

Extinct in the wild; conservation breeding in zoos

Although named the 'Golden Arrow Poison Frog' it is actually classed as a species of toad. It produces enough toxin to kill up to 1,200 mice. Distinctively bright, it has unmistakable black markings against a yellow or golden body. Males wrestle and wave their hands and feet in territorial battles during breeding season. They also possess 'nuptial pads' on the underside of their finger tips to help him grip the female while on top of her back during their breeding season. The last Golden Poison Arrow Frogs, found in Panama, were collected and taken to zoos in an effort to breed them in captivity. Their biggest threats were the chytrid fungus (an infectious disease of amphibians, *Batrachochytrium dendrobatidis*), water pollution and the pet trade.

These organizations are working to save the Golden Arrow Poison Frog:

Houston Zoo

http://www.houstonzoo.org/meet-the-animals/amphibians/

Support the zoo: http://www.houstonzoo.org/support-the-zoo/

The Maryland Zoo in Baltimore

http://www.marylandzoo.org/2014/03/panamanian-golden-frog-conservation/

Donations: http://www.marylandzoo.org/support-the-zoo/

Green and Golden Bell Frog
(Litoria aurea)

Vulnerable and decreasing; endangered in NSW

The Green and Golden Arrow Frog is a diurnal species of tree frog that lives in swamps and ponds. It is bright green with gold or bronze markings on its head and back with a pale underside. With a length of up to 11cm (4.5 inches) the Green and Golden Bell Frog is one of Australia's largest species of frog. They have a big appetite for insects and other invertebrates, and have even been known to eat members of their own species. During the breeding season males will let out a loud, deep growl-like croak while they're floating in water to attract nearby females and warn off other males from its territory. The Green and Golden Bell Frog's dramatic decline is due to the introduction of predatory fish, the chytrid fungus and loss of habitat.

These organizations are working to save the Green and Golden Bell Frog:

FATS – Frog and Tadpole Study Group of NSW Inc

http://www.fats.org.au/en/

Donations: fatsgroupnsw@fats.org.au

Taronga Conservation Society Australia

www.taronga.org.au

Donations:
https://www.thankq.net.au/donate/V269/Donate1.aspx?ref=5609285648&pid=3#make-a-donation

Horned Marsupial Frog
(Gastrotheca cornuta)

Endangered; imminent danger of extinction

A species of frog that lives in trees, the Horned Marsupial Frog has a mottled brown appearance with horn-like protrusions above each eye. It has excellent camouflage in the dense canopy of the forests where it was once found in Costa Rica, Ecuador and Panama. As a marsupial, the female carries fertilised eggs in a pouch on her back right through their development stages until they emerge as fully formed frogs. The endangered Horned Marsupial Frog population is declining due to deforestation for palm oil, the deadly chytrid fungus and pollution from the spraying of illegal crops.

These organizations are working to save the Horned Marsupial Frog:

Amphibian Ark – The New Jambatu Centre for Amphibian Conservation

Donations: http://www.amphibianark.org/donation-jambatu-centre/

Cheyenne Mountain Zoo

http://www.cmzoo.org/

Support the zoo: http://www.cmzoo.org/index.php/support-the-zoo/

Kids Saving the Rainforest – Costa Rica

http://kidssavingtherainforest.org/

Donations: http://www.razoo.com/story/Kids-Saving-The-Rainforest

Smithsonian National Zoological Park

http://nationalzoo.si.edu/SCBI/SpeciesSurvival/AmphibianConservation/

Donations: https://8997.thankyou4caring.org/pages/donations/donate-now

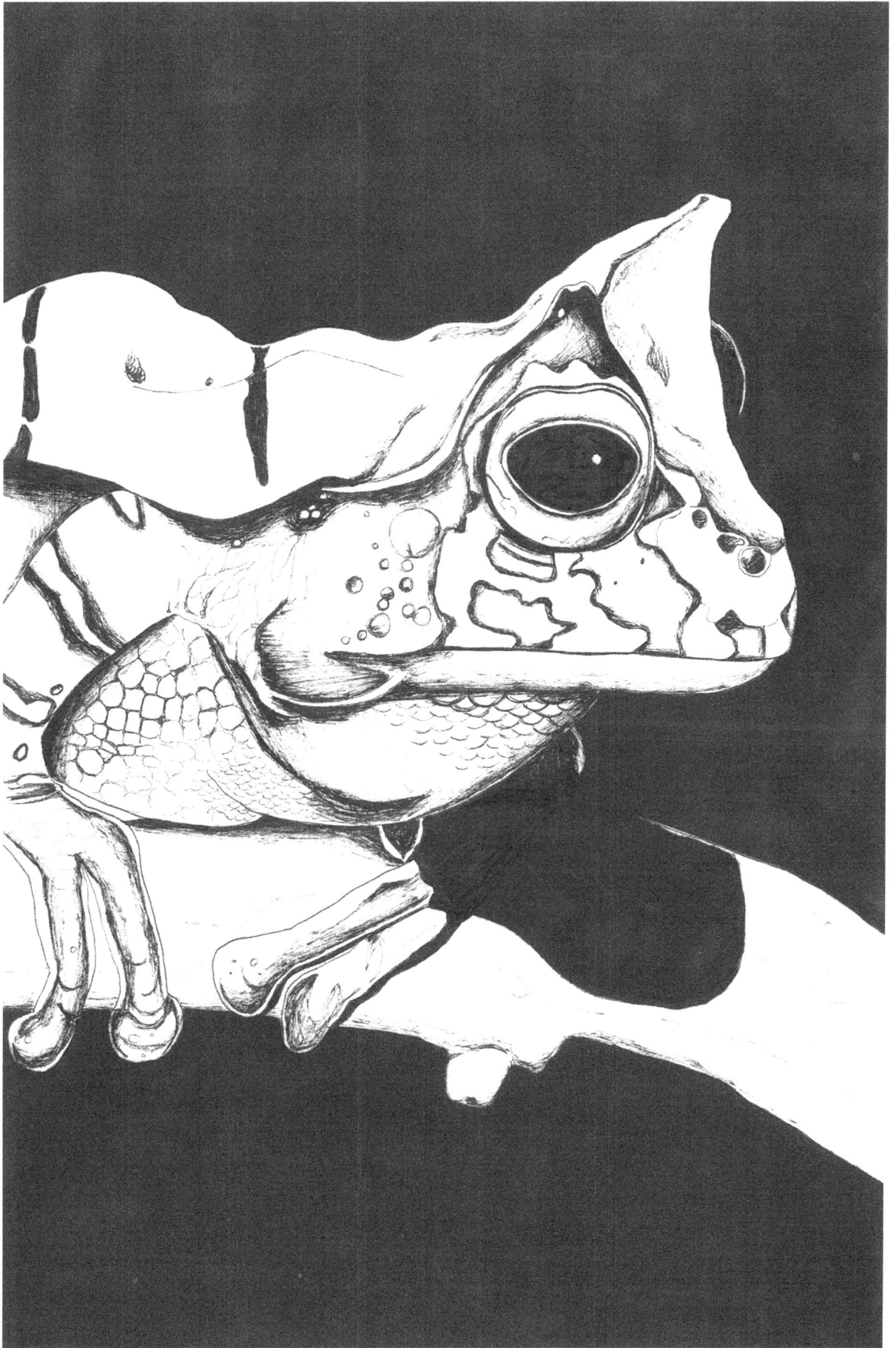

Lake Titicaca Water Frog
(Telmatobius culeus)

Critically Endangered

This giant frog reaches over 5 inches (13cm) from snout to rear, with records of an outstretched length of up to 20 inches (50cm). It weighs up to an impressive 2 pounds (1kg), making this one of the largest aquatic frogs in the world. The many folds of skin over the Lake Titicaca Water Frog's dark green/olive green body, and its greatly reduced lung size, allow it to breathe underwater. It has no need to come to the surface for air which allows it to remain under water in Lake Titicaca. It is endemic to this one lake in the Andes Mountain Range on the border of Peru and Bolivia in South America. It cannot be found anywhere else. This critically endangered species is facing extinction due to its collection for human consumption, habitat reduction and the future threat of the chytrid fungus.

These organizations are working to save the Lake Titicaca Water Frog:

Amazona Zoo

http://www.amazonazoo.co.uk/lake-titicaca-river-frog/

Amazona ZOO, Hall Road, Cromer, Norfolk, United Kingdom NR27 9JG

Telephone: 01263 510 741

Amphibian Ark – the New Jambatu Centre for Amphibian Conservation

http://www.amphibianark.org/titicaca-water-frog-2/

Lemur Leaf Frog
(Hylomantis lemur)

Critically Endangered; population deceasing

The Lemur Leaf Frog is very small and can sit on your fingertip. It is named after the black rings around its eyes that give it a Lemur-like appearance. It is bright green during the day while it's resting and brown when it's active in the night, giving it excellent camouflage within the dense forest. The female lays her eggs on a leaf above water, enabling the tadpoles to drop into the water below and develop into froglets. Threats to the Lemur Leaf Frog include the chytrid fungus, despite its resistance to the disease when compared to other frog species, and also to the ongoing deforestation of its habitat in Costa Rica.

These organizations are working to save the Lemur Leaf Frog:

Amphibian Conservation in Action – Manchester Zoo - Project Lemur Frog

http://lemurfrog.org/

Donations: http://lemurfrog.org/donate/?blogsub=pending#subscribe-blog

Costa Rican Amphibian Research Center

http://cramphibian.com/

Donations: http://cramphibian.com/donate/

Denver Zoo

http://www.denverzoo.org/

Donations: http://www.denverzoo.org/support-us/giving

Macaya Burrowing Frog
(Eleutherodactylus parapelates)

Critically Endangered

Thought to have been long extinct, this brown and dark yellow frog with bright orange flashes on its legs was recently rediscovered in 2010 in Haiti. It still remains critically endangered. The Macaya Burrowing Frog spends much of its time burrowing shallow chambers underground. From here, the males can be heard calling out to females. After mating, the eggs are laid in the burrow and later emerge as froglets, skipping the tadpole stage. While not much is known about this species, and their current population is unknown, their decline is likely due to deforestation through human activity.

These organizations are working to save the Macaya Burrowing Frog:

Caribnature – A nexus for Caribbean nature and conservation awareness

http://www.caribnature.org/essays/eng/index.php?file=save_haiti_frogs

Donations: http://www.caribnature.org/webpages/eng/donate.php

Northern Friends of Haiti

http://www.nfoh.org/

Donations: http://www.nfoh.org/get-involved/donation-form/

Société Audubon Haïti

http://audubonhaiti.org/

Donations: http://audubonhaiti.org/support/donate/

Philadelphia Zoo

http://www.philadelphiazoo.org/Animals/Amphibians.htm

Mountain Chicken Frog
(Leptodactylus fallax)

Critically Endangered

One of the largest frogs in the world, the Mountain Chicken Frog is also one of the most endangered frogs in the world. It gets its name from the taste of its meat. Its colours vary from dark browns to oranges and pale yellows, giving them perfect camouflage to patiently wait for food to pass by. The impressive size of the frog allows it to eat most invertebrates, other frogs and small mammals such as rodents. It can live to be 12 years old. The breeding behaviour of the Mountain Chicken Frog consists of males digging large burrows, up to 20 inches (50cm) deep, into the ground that they will fight over. The winner then calls out to females. The female he mates with will release a liquid that he turns into a frothy substance using his back legs. The female lays her eggs in this froth. Volcanic eruptions, the chytrid fungus, human consumption and habitat destruction on the two islands of Dominica they live on are to blame for this species' critically endangered status.

These organizations are working to save the Mountain Chicken Frog:

Detroit Zoo - National Amphibian Conservation Center

http://www.detroitzoo.org/

A.D.O.P.T.S: http://www.detroitzoo.org/support/adopts

Durrell Wildlife Conservation Trust

http://www.durrell.org/animals/amphibians/mountain-chicken2/

Donations: http://www.durrell.org/donate/
Specify Mountain Chicken Frog in the 'Dedicate My Donation' box or donate by phone +44 (0)1534 860060

Painted Burrowing Frog
(Scaphiophryne gottlebei)

Endangered

An attractively coloured frog, the Painted Burrowing Frog's underside and face are grey with black and it has green and red patterns across the top of its body. It's also called the Malagasy Rainbow Frog and it is endemic to Madagascar. It is a poor swimmer. To avoid drowning in flash floods it has specially formed claws on the front of its feet to help it climb the rocky walls of canyons that surround the dry forests where it lives. It also has a small swelling underneath its feet on its back legs to help it to burrow underground where it spends most of its time. The Painted Burrowing Frog's eggs are laid in shallow rock pools and must develop quickly to prevent being washed away. Although it is considered endangered due to the illegal pet trade, this species has a remarkably high reproduction rate and so all hope is not lost as long as its habitat is not destroyed by human activities.

These organizations are working to save the Painted Burrowing Frog:

Amphibian Specialist Group and the Amphibian Survival Alliance

http://www.amphibians.org/

Donations: http://www.amphibians.org/take-action/

Durrell Wildlife Conservation Trust

http://www.durrell.org/conservation/

Donations: http://www.durrell.org/donate/
Specify Painted Burrowing Frog in the 'Dedicate My Donation' box or donate by phone +44 (0)1534 860060

São Tomé Giant Tree Frog
(Hyperolius thomensis)

Endangered; population decreasing

The largest of the Hyperolius family, the São Tomé Giant Tree Frog is brightly coloured with a green back and an underside that is bright orange with a white and black pattern. It has large toe pads making it an agile climber. It breeds in still water, such as lakes and ponds, on the island of São Tomé. The female lays her eggs in a hole in a tree that has filled with water, high above land. While in this mini-pool in the trees, the eggs develop into tadpoles and then into frogs. The São Tomé Giant Tree Frog is well known for being difficult to find. Little is known about the contributing factors to the decline of this endangered species but the likely causes include habitat loss and the possible threat of chytrid fungus.

These organizations are working to save the Sao Tome Giant Tree Frog:

Island Biodiversity Race

http://islandbiodiversityrace.wildlifedirect.org/

Donate by shopping: http://114726.spreadshirt.com/

Obo National Park

Ecotourism: http://www.obopark.com/

Spikethumb Frog
(Plectrohyla exquisita)

Critically Endangered; population decreasing

There are several variations in colour of the Spikethumb Frog including brown, yellow, and green. It is named after the spike-like digit called a prepollex which is like a thumb. Endemic to only one national park in the Honduras, it lives in low vegetation alongside rivers and is known as a stream-breeding frog. Its tadpoles have lately been recorded in particularly low numbers and scientists think the Spikethumb Frog is likely to be highly susceptible to the chytrid fungus. Both conservation breeding and preservation of its environment are necessary to prevent the Spikethumb Frog from going extinct.

These organizations are working to save the Spikethumb Frog:

Honduran Conservation Coalition

http://www.honduranconservationcoalition.com/

Donations: Honduran Conservation Coalition, care of Mark Bonta
409 West High Street
Bellefonte, PA 16823
USA

Honduras Amphibian Rescue and Conservation Center

http://www.rufford.org/projects/jonathan_kolby

Donations: Hondurasarcc@gmail.com

www.ingramcontent.com/pod-product-compliance
Lightning Source LLC
Chambersburg PA
CBHW081422270326
41931CB00015B/3372